Adobe Odes

Camino del Sol

A Latina and Latino Literary Series

Adobe Odes

Pat Mora

The University of Arizona Press   Tucson

The University of Arizona Press
© 2006 Pat Mora

Library of Congress Cataloging-in-Publication Data appear
on the last printed page of this book.

Publication of this book is made possible in part by
the proceeds of a permanent endowment created with
the assistance of a Challenge Grant from the National
Endowment for the Humanities, a federal agency.

Manufactured in the United States of America on acid-free,
archival-quality paper containing a minimum of 50% post-
consumer waste and processed chlorine free.

11 10 09 08 07 06   6 5 4 3 2 1

For my children,

Bill, Libby, and Cissy,

whose praises I will always sing

Contents

Ode to Adobe

Your blue mouth,
door of a thousand river-rolled stories,
    opens.
Walls whisper,
    voices of earth and straw.

Clay flower,
each of your rooms welcomes
    like a wish,
tastes a different color —
    mango, papaya, persimmon, quince.
In your nichos, Santa Rita and San Judas,
    patron saints of the impossible,
shake their heads,
    gossip
about an aunt's pastel
    lust, while they pretend to pray.

Mud song,
growing to your interior music,
    dream cave,
honey-hive shaped by a choir
    of muddy hands,
ballad of eloquent bricks,
    kitchen of unending banquets,
beans simmering for centuries,

sun-baked loaf, you rise
          from the desert into a luminaria.

     Serenata de barro,
cantadora de la tierra,
          our hands stroke you, wrinkled
               and delicious,
smell the layered legacy
          that shelters us in the arms
                    of candle and piñon smoke.

Your melodies, washed and ironed
          by generations of mothers,
                         drift out,
lure departed spirits home again
          to dream in the crackle
                    of kiva fireplaces
warmed by sips of humor
          and old desires, the taste
               of guacamole, the silk
                    of skin.

     In your candlelit mirror,
eternal vanity:
          a spirit powders her bony nose.

Ode to Guacamole

A guacamaya mashes the chartreuse
    cream
    ripened in darkness,
infusion of sun on the tongue,

seasons the aguacate, the Aztec's ahuacatl
with the Mexican tricolor:
    irrepressible tomato fireworks,
    onion's white bite,
    proclamations of salt,
    streams of lime's tart retorts,
    impetuous pinches
        of chile.

¡Prueba!
parrot-sassy guaca-guacamole.

Ode to Readers

Bien amados,
     hoping you won't slip away,
     and fearing your reluctance to
                      leap
into the web
     of language,
I offer odes simmered for years
     without knowing you.

To lure you,
I've devoured cookbooks
     written en español
by women with a weakness for blue
     roots, canapés garnished with slivers
     of light.
I've gathered what I could reach,
     stirred, concocted,
tasted
     in considerable anticipation.

Try the blood
     of prickly pears,
a woman's silver tears,
rose petals gathered by Sor Juana.

     Snakes slept on my used books,
occasionally offered advice on appetizers,

all starting with the letter
S.
The recipe for guacamole
came from a crow.

Without you,
what I've prepared will wither
into dust.

Tempt you?

Ode to Kitchens

Corazón de la casa,
faithful morning prayer,
sanctuary of seasonings,
    your full face gleams its greeting
lit by yellow lamps,
    lemons and mangos.

Home within my home,
we explore
    your aromatic hiding places,
cabinets, possibilities,
        nests
    of pans and bowls.

Modest celebrant,
spirit of recipes
    stirred slowly into conversations,
with your wood wand,

a worn spoon,
    you wave us into action,
conduct us
        to join your mesmerizing hands,
        beginning the venerable ritual
        of nourishment.

    Amused minister
to our hunger,
while oils and herbs doze,
        you watch us savor
your frayed books,
        secrets
hiding in the leaves.

We borrow your magic
whisks and ladles stuffed deep
        in your apron pockets,
watch your fingers read
        the languages of spices,
combine them into ballads
        that will sing in our skin.

Pots, handled hollows
        hallowed by earth's abundance —
        carrots, onion, potatoes practicing
                arias learned in the shadows —

begin to ring like church bells
        summoning the faithful.
Lids clang their incantations
        in the calligraphy of smoke,
                        incense
of simmering soups—
        lentils, corn, tomatoes,
                scents mingling with yeast's
perfume. Dough's modest chest swells
        with expectation under a cotton cloth.
Warmth works its daily mystery,
        alters elements
into a bouquet of bread.

        Gathered, we feast,
humble temple,
        perpetual family flame,
                muse of metamorphosis.

Ode to Chiles

Always essential
guests at a party,
    chilitos,
flamenco queens
        in your red and green gleam,
¡bienvenidas!

We greet you,
        bevy of beauties,
with a deep, respectful
        bow.
Hungry, we escort you
        to the kitchen,
hold you lightly
        not to bruise your inviting
skin, and frankly fearful
        of your sting.

We nudge the sluggish tomatoes
                to the edge,
but you rub against their plump
blushings,
        bump
into the onion's transparent blouse,

caress
the tangled
        tresses of salacious cilantro
smelling the wild
        in your veins.

The room shines
        with the heat of desire
as the flame loosens
        your tight garment,
                slowly embraces you
                        in its intimate dance
        releases
your smoky, prickly
        perfume.

Chilitos, the humble kitchen board
        becomes your tabla.
Slithery hands peel away
        your wrap . . . black,
                delicate mantillas,
and the clapping begins.

        You rise
dancing in our imagination,
stamping your ripe rhythms,
        el baile delicioso
de la cocina,
el zapateo.

With your flare,
you entangle our tongues
in memories, ensnare
us with the secret
of cooks,
  claim us
    by offering yourselves.

We lose control,
  shove aside
    our firm resolves,
  our ascetic timidity,
and repeatedly we reach
    for ese sabor,
the taste of your blaze,
euphoric captives
  of your sweetgreen
     fire.

Ode to Chocolate

In your smell, our mouths swell
bigger than our bodies,
a slow, hot dance,
      el sueño oscuro,
the wooden spoon stirring
      your melting smoothness
      in a cauldron bigger than the stove.

To escape the gleaming lure, we read
your history, mischievous tempter,
      brown and very American;
      your pre-Pilgrim pedigree.

Botanically, you brew
      our edible mud
in a pod's white pulp.

Rated far above our other native plants—
the almost forgotten amaranth and cassava,
        the common squash, tomatoes,
        maize, and potatoes—
in the continent's culinary genealogy,
        though ordinary-looking seeds,
you were prized more than pineapples,
        avocados, chile, vanilla.

Semillas morenas, once savored
by America's old kings,
        the Olmecs and Maya,
you intoxicated Aztec lords
        with your power.
Hot afternoons, in the temple's shade,
        women rocked back and forth
        over their metates,
ground the toasted and peeled seeds, poured
the powder into pots painted with red ochre,
        clay, charcoal;
flavored the powder with honey,
        chile, maize, vanilla, flowers.
Poured water into the secret, aromatic powder;
        bitter rivers flowing
from pot to pot, into foaming
                        volcanoes.

Columbus saw the seeds traded
as money (that grew on trees),
chewable coins of the realm.
    Tricksters
    filled the empty shells with clay,
    counterfeit caffeine.
The wealthy tossed inferior nuggets to the poor.

You floated to Spain,
    formally presented in European elegance,
    poured into copper and silver pots,
    whirled and twirled with a molinillo
    into a frothy delight.
Butter, rum, caramel, amaretto, Cognac streamed
    into cauldrons bigger than the stove.

Rural and royal cooks and confectioners
still scheme the dusky layers of possibilities —
    an addiction
        sweet and bittersweet —
frosting, fudge, flan, tortes, truffles, kisses,
    devil's food,
        thick, lickable ríos,
the tongue's slow dance.
    Day and night, mouths dream
America's unassuming, dark bean.

Ode to Arroz con Leche

Begin with an illusion
sweet on the tongue,
a mouthful of creamy moon.
Let whimsy take you by the hand
into the kitchen as if you were hypnotized.
Do not resist.

Follow directions,
old rituals
uniting fire and water
into a feverish boiling.
Add curled bark, its fragrance
from India unfurling into an infusion
of memories.
Smell the perfume
cinnamon-scented wisps rising
disappearing
into your hair and wooden spoons.

Extract yourself
from the trance
and add a white stream,
a streak of miniature rice meteors.

Close the lid,
retreat
but listen to water's amorous
            burblings
in the dark, softening
the grains until the liquid vanishes.
Pour more whiteness,
        un sueño blanco, hiss
                of sugar's shimmer,
stubborn salt bits,
        milk's smooth mystery.

Feel the rotation,
        centuries of circular stirrings,
                hands spinning ollas, reveries.

        Simmer comfort,
spoonfuls of bliss.

Ode to Spirits

Daily, you move in me,
    briskly walk through the chambers
of my heart
    and up and down my bones,
greet me in the morning
with quick smiles,
busy with your tasks,
resistant to the pleasures of leisure —
    no tea sipped for hours
        as a book cools in the lap.

    I try to tempt you,
    elusive spirits,
with questions and pan dulce,
        jokes
about the appetite of the dead,
but Mamande, you continue
making beds and Tía Nacha sweeps
the back patio with the spin
    of a whirlwind.
Daddy in white shirt and tie adjusts
    the curvature of a lens,
a working family even in the next phase.

Tía Lola irons
as her ankles swell, teaches
    English to the angelitos
    while stirring steaming pots
of milk and sugar into celestial confections.

Temporarily,
we're all housed in the adobe
        of my skin,
the re-worked mud I am.

        Invisible companions, familia querida,
at night you finally sit
        around the kitchen table,
my grave-defying counselors,
irreverent storytellers
        who carry me back, enfold me
in your weary arms,
        whisper prayers en español,
canciones that echo through my cells
        like the tolling of familiar church bells,
the movement of the holy
        spirit,
                campanitas cantando.

Ode to Names

When parents pour a name
                      over a baby
the way they would pour
                      sweet oil,
rubbing the warmth
        into the fresh skin,
into the chest and limbs,
            pressing the oil lightly into
                baby's closed lids,

when parents pour
        their blessing,
the sounds, a distinctive
        garment,
shelter from anonymity constructed of
        letters, a banner,
            private rhyme,

when parents pour the syllables
        Ma rí a Ig na ci a,
a verbal elixir
created for this one being,
they cannot imagine the pharmacist years later
asking their shy daughter,
        "What's this?
        Ma rí a Ig na ci a.
        That sounds like
        a disease."

On the way home,
the girl folds her name,
        presses
it into a sad speck,
        shoves it deep
                inside herself.

For years, she is
        Mary.

Language, though, is insistent
        as seeds sprouting in cement,
and one day Mary hears herself
        say to her daughter,
        "Soy María Ignacia."

"Speak English, Mommy."

        "Soy María Ignacia,
the ballad of two grandmothers
        who like a river claiming new land
                refuses to be silent,
my grandmothers inside me
        insisting,
                'María Ignacia, canta.
Sing. Sing out our names.'"

Ode to a Book

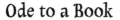

When I open you,
    letters from a stranger
bound for my hands
    from some distant place,
leafed treasure,
sturdy box
    scratched and scarred
        by my journey,

a breeze
    wraps around my shoulders,
pulls me
    to a grandmother dancing
        with her shawl in the dark,
a man eating only carnations.

Like smoke,
a swirl of gray hair
                unravels
its canciones amorosas,
        its mysterious romance,
and a hummingbird dozes on a tiny
cotton puff
        while whirring crimson through its dreams.

Mirrors flow into the street
                          spilling
gossip and beauty secrets.
        Wine-sipping syllables
            chuckle
        over their rhymes.

Pearl of petals,
mi libro, un mundo,
        you open your mouth,
                a bud unfurling,
un canto viejo, fresco, dulce,
sonoro,
        canta, canta.

Ode to Pablo Neruda

Boldly, you hoist your flag,
    Gran Cantador.
Across this earth, this page,
    you stride;
your throat, heart, blood
    proclaiming
lavish love lyrics to potatoes,
    onions, tomatoes,
        canticles to corn.

You motion us to follow
without pausing to count our
money, pack a lunch
    or lock our indigo doors.

We float
down a dirt path on
    your exuberant harmonies,
peer at what you hand us,
    seeds
dreaming of unfolding
    into bark symphonies,
germinating nouns
    sprouting
into revolutionary hymns,
seashells hoarding
    the poetry of waves.

Earthly Troubadour,
    Pastoral Compañero,
you lead us across the sand
                    to the edge,
    to water's secret voice,
and imitating you,
    we remove our shoes and socks,
let the sea lick our skin
    awake with her salty tongue.

Wild grasses brush our ankles
    as we follow you and your flag,
hope flapping in the breeze.

Miner of Jeweled Consonants,
you reach into the pockets
of your baggy pants
and offer us chunks of bread, warm
plums and una canción verde.
Then with an informal hand,
you signal

and safe in your voice,
praise rises
from the soles of our bare feet
like sap climbing
a cottonwood in spring.
Surprised, we hear ourselves,
blushing but bold,
and together we stride on
across America,
polyphonic carolers,
rejoicing
in this glorious earth.

Ode to a Friend

Your voice
    a mischievous breeze trailing
        its aromatic scarf — lilacs, sweet pea —
swooshes its melodies,
and your laugh
    cascades,
        exuberant,
    a joyful río de luz
carries me until I'm floating
    on its rhythm.

    In your funny swing and sway,
I spin in the play
    of your remolino de flores.

Ode to a Cricket

Don Grillo,
at twilight you adjust the tight vest
of your faded tuxedo
and on your wood stage you cough,
slick your hair
with your secret,
flowery pomade,
tune your wings
for their musical flights.

Luring your nocturnal orquesta
with your squeaky persistence,
músico viejo,
you close your eyes
and again play waltzes with the wind,
sonatas with stars,
moon's minuet,
boleros of bumblebees,
turtle tangos,
rondos for a rose.

You drink the night in
until you transform
     yourself
into its insistent song
     and serenade your old love
who hides,
     you hope,
with downcast eyes,
     waiting
       still
in the lacy shadows.

Ode to a Child

Stream of laughter,
you run in
and out
of our breath chasing
the sun
through teasing shadows,
honey flower-tunnels,
between the red and orange mouths
of surprised poppies.

You peer
at a lizard startled into stillness
that some nights grows
in your room, its breathing
bigger than your house,

but you dive into your days,
running dandelion,
scatter questions and tunes
that spin and cling to our clothes.

You bloom on the run,
canción de sol,
tug us to follow
you back
into the grassy world,
the earth-smell,
petal and mud.

Ode to Toes

Elemental buds,
ten essential pudgy acrobats,
daily you balance
our bodies and flabby egos.
Ludicrous, humorous struts,
you support a steep bridge
of bone
and ambition.

Your practical maneuverings,
deditos, your penchant
for digging in the sand,
your totally uncerebral inclinations,
loyal appendages,
keep you playful.
At ninety, though hunched
veterans,
you'll still be little piggies
smiling to be counted.

Do you sing your fantasies
in the shower, drenched choir
of digits?
Romeos tapping secret love messages
even in tight, proper shoes,
or confident exhibitionists
enduring burning
beach sand,

or nervous wrigglers
plotting passion
in scuffed cowboy boots,
or shy under-the-table
nudgers,
tender foot-fingers feeling
tentatively for fellow flesh.

When we type or read,
you rest, grateful
for our sedentary ways,
at dusk burrow into dark
slippers, sleepy mole nubbins,
to catch a nap before the late shift,
the nightly ritual
when we thoughtlessly sleep on our backs,
and you, prop up the sheets —
the wider, maternal toes
bearing most of the weight,
content los chiquitos can doze.

Five and five
miniature Shetland ponies,
soft beasts of our burden,
though you pull a precarious load
toward the west, we ignore you.

Poetic phalanges,
you compose scarlet odes
        to plush carpets
                and slow, orgasmic oil massage.
        Without you,
kings fall flat
        on their startled, regal noses,
or at best, stamp flatly
        without grace or flexibility,
devoid of imperial flare.
        Without you,
ballet and modern dance
cease offering the glittering promise
                                of flight,
and with that lack of elasticity
might we, the more flat-footed,
unable to lift ourselves,
                doubt our reach?

Skin bouquet,
modest extensions
        of distinctive aroma,
                flowering
        of our fragile feet,
perched on high

we salute you.

Ode to Dandelions

Little suns,
exuberant spring heralds,
you wake
    one warm night,
        scurry
on your skinny legs
to decorate the world's fragrant grass,
while we dream in faded sheets
    of violets and daffodils.

You leap
down country roads,
    burrow
under a white wood fence,
    somersault
        across a fancy lawn
into the flowerless yard
of a gray-haired woman
    who sings goodnight
        to her cats.

Proud of your persistence,
deaf to the gossipy whisper,
    "weed,"
you daily grin up at us.

If we yank you out, toss
    you on the compost heap or garbage;

you bloom there too, festoon
egg shells, carrot peels, tortillas and spaghetti.

Modest boutonniere,
you refuse to discriminate
and eyes wide,
        irrepressible yellow rings,
you grow your dreams
in white puffs that sail
        like wild wisps of summer songs
                on which we drift,

shooting stars
back to our past, when free
        of tangled plans,
                we spun
        in your airy plumes
that rooted in our muddy, open hands.

Ode to a Sprite

I conjure you in the garden,
        duendecilla,
daydream my transformation,
an imp among the butterflies, lilies,
        budding hollyhocks.

I hear humming in the buzz
around me, feel strands
of long, black hair
        brush my winter face.

Niñita, no bigger than your furry steed,
you ride a fat bee
        that lands on my big toe.

"Primavera," you chime,
then embarrassed at your glee,
        cover your mouth
                at my boring sobriety.

For a moment, I rest my ear
        on the cloud-pillow of your voice,
                but you skip over to a tulip,

        peer up,
pull off tiny rose slippers,
        stuff them
in your pockets, then hand-over-hand,
        climb

the stem, a skinny,
green dream, a curious
    flute,
an emerald melody,
until you bump your head
    on the soft curve
        of the aromatic wine goblet.

Panting, you slip between
    the petals,
      plop
yourself in a curve, doze
like a kitten in the scented bed
    then stretch
in the sunlight and climb
to a blossom tip, arms high
    slide into the cream heart,
the bloom's startled core,
your hair a halo in the spring light.

    On tiptoes, you lick
the lemon pollen,
wearing *my* face gaze up,
and we're brown eye-to-eye
    wondering
what gravity so impedes my flight.

Ode to a Bumblebee

Portly gorger,
Don Abejarrón,
    weaving
from your clandestine,
rumpled den
    into the morning light,
nodding
    shamefaced,
tipping your battered hat
at disapproving neighbors,
those industrious ants
who shake their heads,
    skinny limbs akimbo
at your laziness,
as you, irresponsible
    tippler,
hoarding forager,
        float again

on your familiar secret
route into
    the irresistible,
the lush, lavender waves
of fragrance, their velvet
    embrace,
        el mar morado.

Fuzzy nuzzler,
    gran maestro,
        zealous guzzler,
you instruct us
in the art of delirious dedication,
    your tongue
so tangled
    in its solitary tango,
its delicious oblivion,
so obsessive,
    so dizzy,

you buzz.

Ode to a Jardín Mexicano

Hint of heaven,
        cielito verde,
roofless room,
walled sanctuary,
you lull us
      when the wind strums
          your bamboo harp,
and the white
    breath
        of orange blossoms
winds around your arches,
rock litanies,
ancient, stubborn prayers.

Your fountain,
massive stone cup,
    spills
        transparent music
into the blue and white
tiled roundness,
melodies of last night's moon,
      celestial magnolia
      floating
in this pool of refreshment,
      liquid poem.

Red-footed pigeons chortle and bustle,
     swallows whistle and skim.
          Our thoughts dart
restless as lizards.

Designed to lure
     us within,
you serenade
the roots
     of bougainvillea's scarlet desire
          climbing to the clouds;
the statue of a saint,
     napping
in the wranglings of orange geraniums,
     arms outstretched,
          hands open,

     the gardener
bending daily
over buds swelling
     in their damp trance.

Ode to Sor Juana

You rose
>   on your words,

>   chased rhymes around
your nursery,
>   a child entranced
by their flitting, flirting colors,
>   teasing shapes.

At three, you opened
>   an old gate,
your grandfather's books
>   and entered a garden
of unending seduction,
>   letters
growing on dusty pages.

Outside, on your knees,
>   you peered
at ruminating bulbs,
>   at seeds sprouting into a cantata,
at vines, also curious,
>   stretching toward light.
Unable to sleep, you'd improvise
>   beneath the sky's wide white eye, dig
leaves that lingered on your fingertips —
>   mint, basil, dill —
simmered in your dreams,
perfumed your cotton pillow.

You swam buoyant
in the mythic and ecclesiastical echoes,
        the turbulent river,
wove sounds, thorny rhymes.
        You drank the garden's music,
violets' velvet whispers,
elegies and eulogies of chrysanthemums,
hyacinths' hallelujahs,
gardenia operas.
        In your habit,
                you hid
and played with a noisy abundance,
arranged sounds in formal combinations,
patterned pathways, verdant riddles,
elaborate topiaries —
        peacocks reciting sonnets,
        parrots proclaiming odes,
anticipating
friends who would stroll
        through your creations,
your meticulous labyrinths,
        tus flores y hojas majestuosas y barrocas,
                bow
to the elegant bouquet, you,
        rosa sonora.

Ode to Words

Country of characters,
bewitching lettered kingdom,
feast of sounds and symbols.

Amor, love,
star gazer,
dancing romantic,
wears a red feather, savors
syllables caramel sweet
on the tongue,
tiptoes around
debts and children's toys
on shiny, old shoes,
spins,
offers purring armfuls
of heather.

Dolor, pain,
frowning miser,
hobbles in,
squeezes, pinches,
twists
our thin, unsuspecting skin
into a purple howl
without even removing
his gray hat.

Gracia, grace,
clever gardener,
orange butterflies hovering
      round her hair and shoulders,
glides
      down dirt roads
      and chipped sidewalks,
offers housekeepers, car mechanics,
cooks and garbage collectors
      armfuls of lilies.

Muerte, death,
persistent mumbler,
      resists confrontation,
her head draped
      in a black mantilla,
         deceivingly shy,
refuses to look us in the eye until
      that last second.

Pluma, feather,
weightless dancer,
      leaps
into the iridescent air and hovers,
      a hummingbird,
distracting, entrancing
gravity with childlike glee.

Verde, green,
stubborn optimist
even in her dark, winter bed,
    dreams
        of the spring morning she'll push
her head through la tierra
    and again be bathed
        in sunlight.

Words: ancient rivers, prisms,
pleasure legacies, delightful noise, prankish
illuminations.

Ode to Our Lady of Guadalupe

Older than our world,
    you hover
patient on a moon sliver
clothed in a mantle
    de hojas y estrellas.

Your skin, Morenita,
mirrors the brown layers,
    bark and roots,
mysterious humus,
earth from which we emerge
    wet and worried.

Full of faith,
    you wait
philosophical about our rivalries
    and earthly revolutions,
confident in circular rhythms,
    epiphanies, evolutions.

    We discover your shade
in the heat of our frettings,
    your limbs
mighty and welcoming,
    a tree sustaining
your impulsive children,

including the wrinkled faces
and squabbling gray beards,
        all who burrow
into the layers of your calm.

Disoriented in our dark doubts,
        we see your aura,
amber in the desert hills.
Your blessing drifts
        over roofs and thorns
as we curl into safe sleep
        covered by the hem of your garment,
                redolent with roses.

We dream a humming tree,
        leafy abrazo,
older than our world
        hovering
                on a silver sliver,
                        incense of tiny stars.

Ode to an Apple

We bite
into your old round
edible myth
set in the extravagant
garden of lullaby-singing snakes
    and kindly bats
who braid our hair,
garnish strands
    with plumeria, jasmine, gardenias.

Your crisp, tasty cycles,
your ruby story
says you stored compressed
        secrets,
mysterious brown specks
    of good and evil
        in your core.
    Fabled tree
you soared on your arrogance,
    your hidden knowledge,
peered down imperiously
    at the canopy of palm trees, ceibas.

We gazed up,
watched you soften,
into a miraculous pink haze,
    blooms like rose butterflies,

an earthly cloud
dreamy with promise, perpetual
        harvests,
the steady temptation,
        globes flaming,
        lanterns beckoning,
        hard hearts
proclaiming their aloofness,
the juicy maturity
        of firm flowers.

On a lazy afternoon
        how could we resist
your forbidden crimson
        scent, your dark lips
in anticipation panting our name
"Eeeeeve."

The first bite best,
a sweet river on the tongue,
        the flesh innocent
until we began to chew
        and felt a hunger,
companion now to the grave.

        With each pregnancy,
we learned more

        about the mystery of heat,
and we experimented
        for generations with seduction,
bathing you
in sugar and butter,
        dustings of cinnamon and nutmeg,
wrapping you in pastry we rolled like legends,
crooning on slow afternoons
        tempting you
                to taste again like the first
transparent bite.

Ode to a Church Bell

Old heart,
bronze, sonorous petal,
acompañadora campana
cantando,
through the ages you've swayed
in your heavy music,
called down cobblestone streets,
entered

the dreams of a child
swinging wide, great arcs,
toes brushing the domed sky
in the jacaranda's lilac shower,

dreams of a bride
gliding again down the aisle
on your echo wearing only
an unending veil,
the breeze breathing
on her skin,

dreams of a woman
sliding
down
your deep, suspended tone,
long, gray hair, her banner
in the impetuous wind.

Musical shell,
chanting contemplative monk,
        little singing cave,
you release
        your round prayers,
                eddying sounds
        drifting through incense
        and morning beams
                of the sleepy church.

        On her crescent moon,
Nuestra Señora
        and her slender smile
                swaying,
        swaying.

Ode to Jesus Laughing

Lying on the scrubby grasses,
drowsy in the sun,
        he listens.

His friends glisten
with sweat, embellish
        the day's tales,
the heaviness of the catch, pulling
        hope's silver
                        glint
into an unsteady boat.

He watches Pedro
        jump up to flaunt the weight
of the net, how he tugged
        until his eyebrows arched,
his whole body now tense
        in the struggle,
and soon the other fishermen,
like children, eager
        for praise, also show him,
with brows furrowed,
        the weight they carried.

    He laughs with them
at splashing stories
        of great, grand fish

larger than boats
still stubbornly swimming the seas,
and finger-sized fishlets
caught in the nets.

Feeling our predictable hunger,
the exaggerations
of his flesh,
he tears the bread he'd warmed
on the rocks for his friends,
chuckles as they eat together,
content
in the daily act
of chewing.

Thirsty, he drinks
from the bottle they offer,
wine in great red gulps,
the grape's drowsy,
hidden transformation.

A breeze meanders
through the olive trees,
and he knits his hands
behind his head,
gazes at the sky,
the blue comfort.

"Are you dreaming
again, Jesus?" Pedro asks,
        and Jesus laughs
at being
        caught again.

Ode to a Cottonwood

Gold flame
    of faith,
light-filled sanctuary,
      autumn plume,
you sway
    a melodic whisper,
soothing as oil.

Bark cathedral,
    soaring symbol,
      fountain of life,
thirsty I enter
    your abundant presence,
      intoxicating shade,

touch your ascending trunk
    rooted flute,
    impulse toward light,

    rough bible,
faith in invisible layers,
    testament
    to the unseen,
    pillar of persistence
and interior celebration,
    marriage of water and sun,
communion of conversions,

narrative
of hope.

I revel
in you, leafy sacrament,
old branching giant,
in your harmony,
hymn of exaltation,
álamo de alabanzas,
the seasonal experiments
of your green-tongued choir.

Earth's cold breath,
rite of survival,
rattle and rasp,
reveals your skeleton,
rhythmic struggle
on this holy ground;
howls, storming heaven
to be heard.

Then the comforting ritual,
la primavera: white wisps,
delicate epiphanies.
Shining shrine,
you glow,
bow and rise,

pattern of grace,
          praising
in murmured meditations
          and antiphons of resurrection,
in the trembling
              reflections
of your tambourines.

Ode to Desire

Beneath a shimmering oak
    releasing its Cincinnati gold,
a man plays his violin.

Through a cold car window
    years ago, I watched
a black man slide his bow, eyes closed.

The tree, a mountain of leaves, rises,
    the duet
rooted and swaying.

Chin on violin,
    standing in an immense fluttering lake,
the man plays his song.

Leaves and years scatter,
    yet unheard music
        rises still,
his eyes closed in desire.

Ode to Play

Down a dark Chicago street
jammed with narrow houses
and cramped cars,
     wires buzz,
lives and voices tangle
in Polish, Spanish, Ukrainian.

Silhouetted, a dream climbs vertically
from a housetop,
created from ordinary wood,
two sticks joined
by a row of rungs,

a hand-made ladder,

desire attached yet ascending,
bird penthouse,
vista,
flirtation with fate,
longing,
crooked puzzle,
illusion,
joke,
wishful escape
     or welcome,
whisper of wings
     on Jacob's angelic steps,

quirky hope.

Ode to Hope

Daily hope rises,
     a radiance streaming
into our white, sleepy
     bones.

From a fiery sphere
     light, like love, journeys,
offers the grace we can bear.

Hope rose long ago
     for your great-grandmother
washing her morning dishes.

With her favorite towel,
     cotton, blue and faded,
she dries the cups and saucers.

She plans a special sugary bit
     to feed her family gathering,
like yours.

By a sunny window, eyes closed,
     she sits and places her hand
on your warm head.

She prays for you,
        a face she never knew
but vaguely imagines—
        all promise.

She counts her blessings,
        the expanding ring
and smiles at the thought of you,
        here, glowing.

Ode to Courage

In this country of strange sounds,
you move quickly
    through your house,
gather clothes, water plants,
una madre bringing order
    to a place you don't understand.

Children slam the door,
    rush to school,
and you sip café con leche
in the sudden quiet
    with your faraway familia de mujeres.

You heat a pot of beans,
    sweep the house,
light a veladora, imagine
    the women here, darning hand-me-downs
in your rooms, their sonrisas
    like steady flames.

    Today their eyes sting you,
pursue you room to room
    fretting
about the bruises.

At night, those spirits hear your daughter
and know her teacher spits the words,
    "Don't speak
that garbage in here."

She pinches
    your niñita when she speaks Spanish,
smacks her with a ruler.

    The woman —
what kind of woman you wonder —
pours hard beans from a bag.
    You hear the beans hit
the wood floor,
    feel the words, "Kneel
on that," hit your daughter's ears
    while the other first-graders
watch the girl who can't talk right.

English tangles in your hair,
    on your tongue,
so you shake the pillows roughly,
    slap the mop down on the kitchen floor.
You see las mujeres.
    Their bodies frown.

    "No entienden.
How can I protect her?
I can't speak English, and my husband says,
    'La maestra is always right.'"

The women stare at you.
Your hija is there now,
    and that teacher's fingers pinch.

Daughter of courage,
you enter the school,
still wearing scuffed slippers,
    your apron faded gray.
You walk through stares,
    see the principal and feel
the familiar hands
    of generations at your back.

You plant your feet
before the suited man
    as if you are sending down roots.
You feel your voice,
their voice, filling you
    and you shake your finger at the man
        as if he's your son.
    "No señor, no señor.
        Hací no tratan a mi'ja."

Your voice and his heart
louder, the principal not understanding —
    and yet understanding —
redder, perspiring, afraid
of a woman who scolds him like his mother
    did when his friends trampled
her tulips and thought it was funny,
    the bruised petals.

By what force, he wonders,
do his mother and this woman
     who will not be stopped
make the earth tremble by shaking a finger?

When you finish, your mouth dry,
     your tongue, a charred wick,
you see again. People stare, ·
     the man stammers.

     You turn,
aproned titan,
seed of hope,
star of freedom,
     and march out.

     At the corner, you allow your tears
finally to slide
     down your face,
       like rain on a weary house.
You comfort yourself
     saying, "Good. Bien."

Ode to Ancianas

You sigh
when the setting sun,
amiga vieja, rubs your backs
with her strong, gnarled hands.
Massaging your shoulders,
her fingertips discover the tensions
of history in your neck,
the centuries of worry.
She presses into the knots
of frustration, releases
your grief and rivers are born.

Your sigh, *ayyyyyyy,*
your crystalline breath,
a glistening ribbon,
floats
through the trees, seeps
into the music of twilight,
sparrows congregating
on a limb of sound,

crickets tuning battered violins,
    the río
serenading the earth that opens
    her tired, fragrant hands.

    In your black shawls, you rest
in your comadres.
    Doña Sol places her hands
on your fierce heads,
    lingers,
her fingers on your indomitable pulse,
    your veins, vines,
night-blooming glimmers.

    You sigh, *ayyyyyyy*,
and settle into yourselves,
    onyx silhouettes,
    proud mountains,
    stubborn shelters,
    circle of wise stones
and again savor your cuentos
    whispered on parched lips
to drowsy cactus.

    Ancianas, black inextinguishable candles,
ebony fountains,
    you rock us in your safe arms,
in the sway of breath and wind.

Ode to El Paso

Stubborn mountain,
rock anchor,
    you grew from cuentos carried at night
in the wind's dry hands,
    seed pebbles
that became your wide-hipped,
unmovable contours, curves
where finches and secretive
    spiders nest.

Poet of ancient seas
and baritone fossils,
    of trilobites and cephalopods,
lyric cantadora of horn corals,
    ammonites and crinoids,

    impatient, gray historian
lured by the whir of a pen,

    its tip, a top whirring,
dancing on the page,
    you write until your fingers cramp
and your shoulders knot,
    weary at the echoes of grief
still moist beneath the boulders
of prejudice.

You wake
stung, eye pierced
    by an angry, red thorn,
        burning struggles,
embedded in your pupil.

    Stern mother,
venerable sentinel, impervious
    to sand thrashings,
you close your face,
    head thrown back,
        you rise rooted in memory,
and when the storm limps away,
        hoarse, gasping,

you hum, unpack your rose shawl
and again toss the lace
    over your bare, wrinkled shoulders,
wear your rippling silver
    bracelet, el río grande.

    Poised to protect,
you sleep standing,
    wrapped in your black rebozo.

    Cada primavera,
lizards play between
    your toes and young again,

you sip the yellow breeze,
      desert fountain of youth,
your breath soft as dawn. You blush
      at the wind's whispered invitations,
at the feathery caresses
      of ruby-throated hummingbirds
      and begin your slow spin.

Your skirts ripple for miles
      encrusted with cactus pads,
magenta cholla flowers, needle-gold spines,
      poppies fluttering like glorious sunsets.

At night, your long, glinting hair streams
      skyward, among the stars.

Ode to Workers

He pulls off his grumbling socks and shoes
    at his kitchen table,
drinks coffee, rubs his hands
    and sore feet, tells them
bedtime stories,
how they'll sleep on vacation,
    stretch to the edges of the bed as if
it were an enormous cloud,
    how he'll wriggle his toes,
settle his head into a pillow and rest,
      float
for a sweet week. Alone, he smiles,
dreams of a place where he doesn't work two jobs,
    where he's the boss maybe,
and his clothes never mutter,
and his feet never ache, and people nod,
    see you,
a city where you don't get up at four a.m.
and ride the bus, or drive your dented car
    to mop, sweep.

While her family sleeps,
a woman pulls on her yawning blouse,
    a woman who irons, presses
to remove her wrinkled worries,
    how she'll pay her bills,
a waitress

who for years has served
her grin.

At factories, fields and fishing boats,
hands half asleep connect wires, pick
strawberries, haul nets.

Ignoring complaints from the soles
        of their feet, trabajadores saw lumber,
open the oven door to remove
        loaf after loaf they're too busy to taste,
kneel planting
        two hundred bulbs for someone else's party.

Roofers, truckers, nurse's aides, miners,
        smudged by the boss's glares.
A cab driver chews daily
        on his stories, a firefighter
shines the truck that hauls
        fear,
women diaper babies of other women.

Barbers, cooks, plumbers, farmers, street cleaners,
men shining
        shoes until they gleam like wet streets,

the woman, hands hot in rubber gloves,
        who cleans toilets all day, polishes mirrors

so I can enter rooms she improves;
women and men
whose backs ache from stooping,
whose joints swell from years
of lifting and lugging the world's garbage,
our heavy greed.

You work, sigh, laugh
and drink café with plenty of sugar
at your table while your family sleeps;
croon another vacation story
to your aching hands and feet
as if they were your tired children,
whisper, "We'll stroll
on warm sand like in the movies,
and play in the blessings of the sea."

Ode to Rain

Earth blessing,
vertical river of memories,
    impetuous refreshment,
you grace us
    with your pine and aspen harmony.

Like a cascade of coins,
    you dance
staccato on tin rooftops,
    cry on the windowpane
with a man staring
    at a fading photograph,
whisper a lullaby
    to a woman dreaming
herself, a child again
    strutting
through a desert shower
    festooned in damp diamonds.

Liquid caress,
you wake hollyhocks
    from their parched, dusty sleep,
into the tangle of fertility.

Silver language,
you slide and rise,
    gather and release,
instruct us in your circular practice
    of abundance, greening the earth.

Ode to a Desert Willow

When you sprouted,
prickly pear and sagebrush
      stared
at your odd arms, offered
their protection and advice.
Innocent, you dreamed
      of thick-chested grandparents
with wide, expansive arms
      who sang operas day and night
and looked nothing like
      your squat, needle-nosed neighbors.

Embarrassed by your uncontrollable height,
      you stuttered with surprise
when the wind began his daily visits,
      whispered
that you were entrancing,
        that he discovered songs
he sang only in your limbs.

Your solo improvisations
      attracted bees and butterflies.
Birds arrived to enjoy
      the view, your expanding verandas.
News spread that choirs gathered
      at dusk, young pajaritos
          climbing
with you into the clouds.

Árbol solo, anchored dancer,
    loyal survivor of doubt, drought
      and difference,
shelter, soughing oasis.
    You ascend
      arms open,
accepting what arrives
    into your emerald embrace.

Ode to Sunflowers

Curious little rounds,
like your mother, Doña Sol,
    you also rise from the dark.
Inquisitive,
    you lean forward,
eager gazers
    who tint the wind
yellow with exuberance.

In Spain, I watched you,
    like fields of gold moths
        mirasoles meneándose.
Quizzical canaries,
    you crane your slender necks,
stare up in fascination
    at our burning ball of faithful light.
Freed of roots and stems,
        you'd fly,
    burst into flutters of wild abandon.

Bees, like fat professors,
    frown and for hours explore
your persistent optimism, poke and peer.

Patient, you tolerate their scrutiny, wonder
        at their sober reluctance to remove their
striped coats and savor
        your innocent, anchored joy.

In autumn, broody season,
        garden conversations turn philosophical,
leaves pontificating on life's brevity, the weight
        of maturity. Seed-heavy, your head bows.

Ode to Santa Fe

Like a pilgrim, I journey
anxious for the sight and scent
    of your brown garment.
I find you in the hills,
    Old Spirit,
trudging along, exploring
    a duet with a raven,
shaking your head at skittish quail
    that scurry
under the folds of your long, patched skirt.

You open your arms wide
    when you see me and lift me
        from all I carry, swoop me up
into your glorious light.

You take my hand,
pull me along
    accompanied by your old lover,
        the wind, tu músico,
           who strums wild grasses
with his long, bony fingers,
    serenades us
by fiddling on dry cholla stems,
    whistles through yucca pods,
        drums an old aspen
and for a grand finale
    conducts cottonwoods' hushed carols.

We study the mountains, meditating
        in their cloud shawls,
                rising,
their stern habit, undaunted
        even by the bravado of thunderstorms.

From your deep pockets,
        you offer handfuls of seeds, fling
them out with a wide arc,
        teach me to stretch my arm for miles,
hoarding nothing.

        You kneel,
put your ear low
        to hear the arroyo's newest
composition, the daily incorporation
        of sky, leaves, the murmurings
of minnows and tadpoles,
        the liquid lyric.

You shape new hills,
        hollow a small cave,
furnish it with dry branches
        and pink plumes for a fox hunting
a new home, a quiet place to curl
        into the extravagance of his tail.

Ignoring my subtle suggestions
      that we rest, on you stride,
            deeper into the earth's old story,
fingering fossils and myths,
      in the pine's perfume

      Solitary woman, philosopher of silence,
brown caress,
      vessel of light,
      after sunset, you point to the stars
I haven't seen in months,
and to los espíritus
      who wander a land they refuse to leave.

Ode to St. Francis of Assisi

Il Poverello, your hands
naturally curve into nests.
    Your body opens
into a tree, *una pensione* for wrens, crows,
        magpies tired of flight and hungry
for conversation.

    Protector of the ignored,
you scoop a brown worm
        struggling up the rocky road,
                and place it on a shady patch
of grass, release the skinny radiance
        of your weary brother
                tenderly into the cool greenness
as if he were a prized canary
        warbling his joy.

Knees scraped and rough, you teach
        yourself to hear
melodic murmurs below the noise,
        earth lullabies
that sway cats into luxurious naps.
        You hear rocks chant,
and when bees' parched winter hymns begin,
you order honey and wine for the thirsty,
        winged choir.

Your canticles enter
        animal fur and wool.

At the cave at Greccio,
　　　ox and donkey arrange themselves,
supporting actors at your live Manger.

At Gubbio, even the blood-guzzling
　　　monster, *il lupo*
who rushes toward you
　　　teeth sharp
　　　　　　in anticipation
stops.

Your hand blesses him
　　　with the Sign of the Cross.
Your fingers float
　　　before his eyes, hungry
　　　　　　　like yours,
and his teeth retreat
　　　into his gums.
His eyes drink in gulps from the well
　　　of your peace, and he kneels,
places his paw on your hand.
　　　Silently, you comfort one another.

　　　Sometimes reluctantly, you submit
to earth's bounteous affection:
　　　a falcon, devoted butler,
　　　　　watches you sleep

but wakes you,
    kek, kek, kek,
when you're rested;
    a pheasant who, much as you resist,
stubbornly carries the hem of your robe
      in her proud beak;
    a lamb trotting behind you, grinning up
at your frowns.

    Antiphonal minstrel,
flesh song,
    you sing back to the world,
      answer a nightingale.
In a brown-robed duet,
    you chant the Hours.
In Portiuncula, a cicada calls
    from a tree outside your cell,
      and your mingled praise
ripens figs into soft, purple globes.

    Not that you sing your life away,
dolce trovatore di Dio.
    You preach to all creation
      including fish and flowers.
You hush swallows' chirps and twitters,
    the frog chorus interrupting
      words burning your mouth.

Yet animals flock
to you, body of nectar.
	A lark settles on your head.
Robins nuzzle your beard.
	A hen and her brood seek you
through poppies and buttercups,
nestle around your feet.

Ode to Miracles

How does the air sound
around a saint?
    Do the attentive hear
             a faint trill,
a tremor in the breeze,
or is it a scent,
    holiness,

not incense or candle smoke,
    but the heavenly fragrance
of a moon in bloom.

Milagros might have occurred
on every hill, *girasoli* cheerfully following
    St. Francis through olive trees,
        cypress tapers flickering in gold
          -green Umbrian light.

Would the blind cat have known,
    and does she know now
and watch you,
    with clear turquoise eyes,
        waiting for you
to fully appear?

Ode to Another Chance

Your eyes shut, and your mind
                                drifts
        to the inner dark,
a circular miracle,
        the mystery:
your self who speaks in your dreams.

A man's voice on the radio
                                intrudes, pulls
you out roughly, extracts you
from your slumber with the morning news —
                                flags, bombs.

        Light slides into your room,
a melody,
        comforting, familiar, like a mother's
perfume,
        eases you back from the dark.

        Briefly you believe
the blue world waits, needs you,
        but you linger, curled again
                in the cocoon
of sheets your body warmed.
        You yawn,
wrapped in your old habits.

        Each day, we rise, reborn,
our round rhythm:
                another chance.

Ode to Skin

     Permanent costume,
you and I slid into this old earth
                    together, bound
for life.
       You stretched with me, perfect fit,
unique scented envelope,
     delicate yet sturdy
          layers of protective peel,
smooth, human silk.

     You feel the world for me,
linen of leaves, bark riddles,
flesh mystery of children,
comfort of sheets
            that wrinkle, like you,
our creased testaments
          to earth's gravity.

     With your natural inclination
for healing and closure,
     you preserve my autonomy
in this soft, cell-made cell,
     separate me,
          my anatomical self
even from me —
those inner, bloody wonders, loyal lungs,
     practical corazón pumping its blue
yearnings,

the skull
                    staring
behind you, snug mask,
at a skeletal world of identical
          brothers and sisters,
the communion of bones.

          Wise, crinkled sheath,
refusing to be timeless,
                              through the years
you begin to detach;
          hug me with less intensity,
relax and
                    sag into afternoon reveries,
indifferent
to images of bodily perfection.
          Comfortable at being dated,
a disappearing garment, you become
                              more transparent,
reveal a classic design
of thin, veined rivers.
          Quietly demanding, you request
                                        loyalty.

          I watched my mother
in her eighties coo

to herself in the mirror,
and later, as she instructed,
    I watch you, my familiar disguise,
crease with delight
        at my whispered endearments.

Ode to Women

Listen to the place where life grows,
      the inner seedbed
of music
         that curls and branches.

Women's hum of hope
      careens down canyons,
         skims the tops of pines,
the sound of luna's long fingers stroking
      a child's cheek or pouring
clear tea into the fragile cup
      of an old woman.

Listen to the hum
         that sweeps despair
into a battered dustpan
         and flings the gray
tangles out the door,
that simmers a wild abundance
         of summer pears.

The twilight lullaby sways
      forests, mountains, cactus,
homes struggling to stand in the dark;
      the hum
sways women weary from holding
         together a family
of elbows and sighing skin.

Listen to its jazzy improvisations
                    luring, pulling
reluctant hands across borders,
        shore to shore carrying bodies
over choppy waves of fear
                    on its sturdy song.
The hum soothes wounds
        with a mysterious melody that nestles
                in the soul and harvests discarded
stories, knits their threads
                    into a shawl.

Listen, for when mujeres gather,
        O when women gather
to hold hands together,
        their hums rise and ripple, sway
like candles, a symphony
                    of light.
The polyphonic harmony
melts bruises, guns, locks
rusted for centuries,
        the hum of hope swells,
                        sails
across restless seas,
gathers and rocks the globe.

        Women,
the world's stubborn, triumphant hum.

Ode to Tulips

Coy you arrive,
slender girls, silent and proud
in your fluted finery,
                            gliding up
undulations of air
                    toward the light.

A whisper of red
    in your oval heads
hints at your hidden
                        rubies,
but lips pressed,
you suppress the untimely appearance
of your heart.

Petaled egg,
privately you smile, savor
your hidden beginnings,
the worms' nocturnal stories
            stretching through melting snow,
the industrious efficiencies
        of ants, the rushed
brushings of their tiny feet
                    around the coiled dream
that nourished your slender journey,

the paradox:
        protected possibilities
and irrepressible sprouting.

     Your laugh
so deep in your throat
           I have to hover

to hear, rises, opens
          your seven crimson secrets
to a yellow sunrise within,
     as it is in all of us,

     the yolk
     golden bell
     exuberant wick
          the flare of our particular light.

Ode to Lemons

    Kitchen lantern,
fragrant orb,
I wake to your yellow glow,
your concentrated
     brewing,
the inwardness of prayer,
outpourings
         of clear radiance.

    Miniature castle,
you open to reveal your triangular cells
encrusted with pale, scented
     jewels,
liquid slivers
       rivulets of tart light
transforming my tea into an amber pond
with your sustained hum.

    Palm-sized pitcher,
with your habitual resolve,
you dissolve
      the hard edges
of sugar crystals
        into a fragrant syrup.

You perfume thick batter,
      eggs and flour
that rises, floats on a yeasty
      melody.

Even at rest, haloed oval,
you purify the air,
                modest sun,
little canary nun.
      Silently you beckon,
cheerful beacon.

Ode to Tea

Ruminating leaves and blooms,
in solitude you ponder,
    brood.
Steeping, you expand,
     sleepy in your own fragrance.

Scents stream up
          the wispy steam,
and we float too in the flowery mists,
the ritual older than history,
    cup of comfort,
tonic affordable for generations,
    sympathetic companion
who never argues or contradicts,
ancient cure, transformative
    elixir
for cold, loneliness, pangs
          of the heart.

Pozito de paciencia,
    round the world we sip
your philosophical tranquility,
our worries and aches eased
        by your contained calm,
pool of reverie, spring
     of energy, petite reservoir
of wisdom.

Ode to a Pond

Ojo verde,
third eye open in the desert,
smooth jewel on earth's finger,
swirling cup of life,
you pull
    me into your unending whirls,
hypnotize
    with trees extending their trunks
down into the bloom
    of underwater branches.
Mysteries and murmurs
    revolve in you,
        splashes of revelations.

Moist mirror,
you lure me
    down into a liquid world,
        the tonic of inversions,
pink floating dahlias rising
    into stems that blossom into rocks,
ripple
    los alabados a la mañana.

You resist nothing,
accept what appears,
    delicate, a dream that echoes
        in circles, the world's roundness,

quivering like a canary's trill,
unfolding like a peony.
　　Your transparent skin
vibrates with the earth's sigh,
with fish fin, dragonfly wing.

Below the surface, fragile
as sleep, sueño rodando, rodando,
a thousand minnows glide
　　　　　　　　　　through
　　　　stones, lilies, reeds,
　　　　　　　caverns and castles,
the gold
　　　fish rising like a memory,
a sunset in India,
　　　　　the blaze again.

Afternoons, you cast your shimmers,
　　　light rehearsals played on trees.
At twilight, la luna turns
　　　　　　　　　her head slightly,
wise, but still curious,
stares
　　　down at you,
at earth's emerald rings,
reflections of her full face.

A bullfrog rolls

          in moon's white melodies,

in the aria that softens

mountains, en la alegría

       de agua y luz,

and Señor Rana's raspy

          throat fills with riotous,

irrepressible praise.

Ode to Clouds

Water dreams,
        you stream on the waves
of the world's currents,
      round us you float, uncoil
into a dancer stretching
          her slender legs
until they dissolve
         into her music.

Puffed, you gather
        into sea goddesses
fluffing masses of white curls,
your deep, gray eyes staring down
          bemused at our heaviness.

Carefree, you flip,
       delight in your transformations,
become parrots winking impudently
         at Don Sol.

The more flamboyant
            slide
toward the sun when it sets,
absorb his disappearing ardor,
select your evening attire,
     a pink scarf for the demure,
       papaya turban and matching kimono
for the triumphant turning gold in the finale.

The more meditative glide
                    in silence
to the cooler heavens,
light your lanterns
and mumbling read in gray robes or brood purple
        contemplations
            of salvations, revolutions.
Nubes jugadoras y soñadoras,
                you entertain us,
        frolic
in the glorious blue arc of our days,
visible mutations,
        celestial horoscope,
                reliable as our palms, tea leaves
        or Greek coffee grounds.
You stage comedy and omens,

the sea's reveries
        visible and streaming
as she rolls over
        in her dreams.

Ode to the Earth

Above the churning river, out on a flat slab,
an easel, two chairs, two bundled women
        hold chopsticks on a cold afternoon;
ignore the tourist swirl, the posings
        of black, gray and brown lampshade hats.
The couple enjoys privacy, warm rice,
        admires both the roiling, silver-blue
currents careening toward them,
                                zig-
        zagging, lunging at boulders, crashing—
and drying still in their painting.

Tourists startle me
                coming down the path
shouldering their supplies in the early morning.
        Guns? Even in this Asian haven?
No—tripods, cameras, held by bowing admirers
        of rowan trees, imperial birch trunks.

Only the lapping of the crater lake,
        its explosive history visible
in the fiery leaves. A crow caws here
        and in Santa Fe the same sun sets
behind a mountain, lights thousands of insects
        whirling into a cloudy column of glitter.
A lone spider thread
                glistens
between earth and sky.
                        Far below,
springs fill the lake with stars.
        We listen to the soft splashes
on lava stones and beech limbs, hushed
        blessings sliding endlessly toward us.

Ode to a Kiva Fireplace

In the corner of the room,
wrapped in your worn, black shawl,
you sit, a bundle,
lips pursed,
all day feigning sleep
but memorizing
our stories, combining
and stirring them slowly into
your verbal soups,
salsas, flan.

When la luna rises, viejita,
you wait for us to gather around you,
and voice crackling,
you begin.

Your long fingers toss
light and dancing shapes,
witches with pointed hats,
fireflies in their hair,
hike their skirts and dance
"El jarabe tapatio" played by a tree
once struck by lightning.

Ravens in top hats tap dance
on your shoulders,

juggle gold
    coins tossed high into
the secret portal,
    magic tunnel,
    your cueva de cuentos.

    Tattling ghost tongues
repeat rumors of kisses
    tart as pomegranates that burn
the mouth for decades.

    A woman galloping alone
        in the moonlight,
her long hair whipping in the wind, races
    toward us, eyes wide. As we duck
      to avoid her,
        her hair brushes
our cheeks, and at the pine smell
        in her palms, we're off,
riding with her through
  adobe walls, stars popping
around us, dusting
    our skin with sparks
      that drift into our
bones, seeds of light
      waiting for another cold night
      to open
their shimmering mouths
    and continue the tale.

All night, Old Woman,
dark, desert songbird,
grillo de la buena suerte,
spinner of sturdy letter threads,
wrinkled enchantress,
your fingers weave shapes and shadows
until our eyes close, your voice
carrying us on its rhythm.

Sleepy, you begin to nod,
fold your hands
into your shawl, alone —
and not alone —
fold into yourself,
head bowed.

Acknowledgments

My thanks to the editors of the publications in which versions of these poems previously appeared:

"Ode to Ancianas" and "Ode to a Church Bell," *Tex: A Magazine of Texas Fiction, Poetry and Art*

"Ode to the Apple," and "Ode to Hope," *Spirituality & Health*

"Ode to a Child," *Borderlands: Texas Poetry Review*

"Ode to Courage," *Margie: The American Journal of Poetry*

"Ode to El Paso," and "Ode to My Spirits," *Puentes: El cuento en la frontera*

"Ode to Jesus Laughing," *Solo 5: A Journal of Poetry*

"Ode to Women," *Science of Caring*

I also wish to express my deep appreciation to the following: my family and friends for their steady faith and support; my agent, Elizabeth Harding; Tey Diana Rebolledo and the 1999 Pellicer-Frost Bi-national Poetry Award; a Civitella Ranieri Fellowship; friends Murray Bodo, John Drury and Norma Jenckes who read an early draft; the manuscript reviewers for their kindness and advice; the fine staff of the University of Arizona Press; the Honors Program at the University of New Mexico where the poems began; and to Professor Yoshinori Yasuda, who afforded me the opportunity to savor the final editing by Lake Towada, Japan, a feast of beauty.

Other Books by Pat Mora

Poetry
Aunt Carmen's Book of Practical Saints
Agua Santa: Holy Water
Communion
Borders
Chants

Nonfiction
House of Houses
Nepantla: Essays from the Land in the Middle

Young Adult and Children's Books
*Doña Flor: A Tall Tale about a Giant Woman with a Great
    Big Heart*
The Song of Francis and the Animals
A Library for Juana: The World of Sor Juana Inés
Maria Paints the Hills
*My Own True Name: New and Selected Poems for Young
    Adults*
Love to Mamá: A Tribute to Mothers (editor)
Delicious Hullabaloo / Pachanga deliciosa
This Big Sky
Uno, Dos, Tres: One, Two, Three
Confetti: Poems for Children
The Desert Is My Mother / El desierto es mi madre
The Bakery Lady / La señora de la panadería
The Race of Toad and Deer
The Night the Moon Fell
The Rainbow Tulip

Tomás and the Library Lady
The Gift of the Poinsettia / El regalo de la flor de
  Nochebuena, with Charles Ramírez Berg
Pablo's Tree
Listen to the Desert: Oye al desierto
Agua, Agua, Agua
A Birthday Basket for Tía

Library of Congress Cataloging-in-Publication Data
Mora, Pat.
  Adobe odes / Pat Mora.
     p. cm. — (Camino del sol)
     ISBN-13: 978-0-8165-2609-3 (acid-free paper)
     ISBN-10: 0-8165-2609-5 (acid-free paper)
     ISBN-13: 978-0-8165-2610-9 (pbk. : acid-free paper)
     ISBN-10: 0-8165-2610-9 (pbk. : acid-free paper)
     I. Title.
  PS3563.O73A66 2006
  811´.54—dc22
                                    2006018873